MAINE SAMPLER

Harvested by Bill Sawyer

A Collection of

Maine Humor

DOWN EAST BOOKS

Cover design by Larry Zwart

Copyright © 1982 by William P. Sawyer
Cover illustration © 1990 by Lawrence Jan Zwart
ISBN 0-89272-215-0

Printed and bound at Camden Printing

DE   10   9   8   7   6

Down East Books
P.O. Box 679
Camden, Maine   04843

For

my wife, Dorothy, my four children—Judy, Bill, Jr., Nancy, and Janet—and my eleven grandchildren.

And last, I pass this bit of heritage on to my sister Betty Secrist and in memory of my younger sister, Lucy, who grew up with me on that saltwater farm on Little Chebeague Island in Casco Bay. I can picture today Lucy, whose auburn curls could be seen bobbing along in the meadows of buttercups, Queen Anne's lace, and devil's paintbrush, as she ran after her older brother and sister calling, "Wait for me."

WHY THIS BOOK?

The Maine stream flows in the blood of all you children, unfortunately not in your mother or grandmother as the case may be. Upon marriage, she was a dyed-in-the-wool outlander from someplace west of Bangor called Milwaukee. However, by osmosis from old Chumslick and a fairly steady diet through the years of good Maine air, she has come around pretty good and is now almost accepted despite the misfortune of her birthplace.

The State of Maine is more a state of mind than an area. No place in this nation can compare with Maine in terms of its air, coastline, mountains, lakes, fog, smells, bayberry, new-mown hay, clam flats, potatoes, blueberries, and most of all, its people.

When some say a State of Mainer is solid, that's just what he is—all wool and a yard wide. Since Day One, he or she has been as independent and self-reliant as an Eskimo. Each Mainer's lifestyle is as simple as it is complicated and diversified. *He* is a fisherman, boatbuilder, farmer, veterinarian, carpenter, plumber, mechanic, woodsman; *he* is everything unto himself. *She* is a lady, mother, cook, doctor, teacher, diplomat, minister, field hand, pot hauler; name it, *she's* it.

In thought and speech, the Mainer is direct and always on the target. Time is precious, and there is no sloshing around. Get at it, and get it done. Some may say a Mainer is apt to be stoic. Maybe so, since all emotions—whether happy or sad, angry or mirthful—are held pretty much within.

Maine humor and jokes are really just manifestations of a rare directness with which few people are blessed. Because of its arrow-like course, the native tuning of the language, and the short, concise speech mixed with equally rare perceptiveness, the Mainer becomes funny to most outlanders. And though in most cases he does not mean to be, he is just that: FUNNY.

Gathered together here are some of the so-called jokes I have heard over a lifetime as man and boy, growing up summers on a saltwater farm on Little Chebeague, fishing and cruising the length of the coast, pulling kale on a potato farm, and mildly glimpsing culture and learning at Bowdoin College. Most have been heard in the original, a few are old hat and threadbare from being kicked around in books and records in tourist traps; a couple come from the Vineyard. To me, all are fun and worthy of collection.

A SAMPLER OF MAINE HUMOR

While buying some lobsters from Elroy Johnson on Bailey's Island, I asked Elroy how the world was treating him.

He put another lobster on the scale, looked me real good, and said, "Seldom."

———

Two old timers were sitting in front of Alley's General Store watching the folks go by. One leaned over and said, "'Spose there's as much oogy-poogy goin' on as there used ter be?"

"Yep, but it ain't same folks doing it."

Aunt Helen McCoy's family moved for a few summers from Little Chebeague to Buck Harbor on the Eggemoggin Reach.

During the first summer, Aunt Helen's grandfather died. They buried him on a knoll up behind the barn—white picket fence, stone, and all.

Seems that following winter the railroad was extending its line further east and was going right through where Grampa was buried. One of the road's executives called Aunt Helen to see if she could get the grave moved over. She was in Philadelphia and called a fellow in Buck Harbor who agreed to do the job.

Upon arrival the following summer, she asked him, "Did you get Grampa moved over?"

"Ayah."

"By chance when you was moving him, did the casket break open?"

"Ayah."

"Did you see Grampa?"

"Ayah."

"How'd he look?"

"Peaked."

Aunt Helen told me that once as a youngster she was traveling on the railroad from Portland to Camden. In those days there was only one track, and when the train arrived in Camden, the engine was put on a "turnaround" at the harbor and headed back to Portland. A young gal was sitting across the aisle. When the conductor came by the girl stopped him and asked, "Does this train stop at Camden?"

He gave her a real icy stare and kept going down the car. Next time he came by, the same thing happened. The third time he came by, she grabbed ahold of his coat, shook it and asked again.

He looked at her real hard and said, "Well, if it don't, you're going to get the worst ducking you ever got."

Some time back a former hand of mine from up-island was leaning over a fence with a mate of his who had come ashore to go famine. They were gamming and looking at a horse grazing in the pasture. Suddenly the horse came about fast and dropped dead. The owner said, "Gol darn, if that ain't the first time I ever seen her do that."

One summer I went lobstering with Cap'n Alfred. We hadn't gone swordfishing that summer as the Russians had got all the bait and there were very few swords to iron.

One morning I was driving up to the Head from down-island and had forgot my watch. There was a fellow up Tisbury-way mowing his lawn with one of those old pusher mowers. He was running, and sweating, and pushing like all get out.

I stopped and asked him what time it was.

He kept pushing and said, "I ain't got no time for time today."

It was the end of August. A summer visitor walked into Alley's store and, while getting some groceries, said, "You got a lot of queer people around here."

"Won't have after Labor Day."

3

One night I asked Alfred what kind of day he'd had.

"Damn it all, Bill, I've been so Christly busy, I ain't got a thing done."

———

A few years ago we were cruising down east in my Novi sword-fisherman, the *Cachalot*. We put in overnight to visit with some friends in Cundy's Harbor in Casco Bay. After years of navigation with only a compass and a depth finder, I had finally gathered together enough money to install a radar, loran, digital-recording depth finder, C.B. radio, and so forth.

One of my old friends, a lobster and blue fin tuna ("hoss mackerel") fisherman, came aboard and carefully examined all the new equipment. He finally said, "Lord Harry, Bill, you sure got some mighty fine gear aboard here. Must of taken a pile of money. Think it would have been better to jest get a 'fogauger.'"

I said, "Christ, I never heard of a 'fogauger.' What in Sam Hill be that?"

He said, "Well, just a right fine brace and with a six-inch auger. All you do is bore a hole clean through the fog dead ahead, and you can see where you're going. Finest kind."

Those fellows will pull your leg plumb out of the socket if you're not careful.

———

Another time we were tied up alongside a dock in Northeast Harbor. It was dead low tide. On the other side of the pier a fancy sailing craft from New York was keeled over and some fellows were working around the propeller. An old-timer was leaning over the rail watching them. One of the New Yorkers yelled up to him, "Say, what do you guys use in your stuffing boxes?"

The old-timer yelled down, "Peanut butta."

———

An outlander pulled up to the curb and said, "Can I take this road to Portland?"

"Guess you can. But I figure they got plenty of them up there."

———

Asked a fellow in Jonesport if he'd lived there all his life.
"Not yet," he said.

———

A summer visitor stopped into the local store in Damariscotta
just before Labor Day. The owner was sitting by the pot-bellied
stove mending a God-awful mess of gear. The visitor said, "Well,
we're leaving tomorrow. Guess most of the summer people will
too. What are you going to do all winter?"

He let one go in the general direction of the old brass spittoon
and said, "Fumigate."

———

Cruising in a Friendship sloop down east, somewhere off Port Clyde, we hit real thick o' fog, and damned if we could hear or see the bell buoy at the entrance to the harbor.

We heard a lobster boat chugging along and made for the sound. When we finally fetched him, we yelled over, "Pretty thick fog!" He yelled back, "Ain't so bad if you know where you're goin'!" and off he gunned her and was out of hearing before we could catch him.

Some years ago a fellow took his wife lobstering with him. There was a heavy sea running in the same type of "thick o' fog."

Seems she fell overboard, was washed away, and drowned.

Week or two later, a couple of fellows were hauling their traps and up she come!

They called the widower, gave him the news, asked him what they should do with her, and added that when they hauled her she had eight lobsters hangin' on her.

"Eight lobsters!" he said. "Bring them up to the house and set her out again!"

Henry Bailey tended the drawbridge over to Wiscasset. Henry had his hat in the ring for selectman. A friend of his, Hiram, heard that a third friend, Bert, wasn't going to vote for Henry.

He went to Bert and said,

"I hears you ain't gonna vote for Henry."

"Nope."

"Why not?"

"Killed my cow."

"God, how'd he do that?"

"Drowned her."

"Jesus, what happened?"

"Wall, Bess was ailin' some and me and the wife called the vet. He says warn't nawthin' 'tall. Jess flush her out with warm water chock fulla soapsuds.

"Wife and I looked 'round the barn to find a funnel or somethin', and all we could find was son's old bugle. We got Bess half full.

She didn't like it a mite, broke loose, and honked out the barn hell bent down the road toward Henry's drawbridge. Damned fool Henry opened the draw, and Bess kept right on course and off into the river.

"Wall, I'll tell you, any fella doesn't know the difference between the blast of the mail boat and a bugle up a cow's ass don't have brains enough to be selectman."

———

While I dangled my legs over the end of a pier in Casco Bay with a couple of islanders, a teenage summer fellow (outlander) kept circling the harbor in a real fast outboard. There was a submerged ledge just off the pier. Each time he went by us he would just miss the ledge. Finally, one of the fellows leaned over to the other and said, "He'll fetch it next time."

———

While hunting in the deep woods of Canada one year, I met a French-Indian mink trapper. I asked him how things were going. He replied, "Well, if I don't do better last year than I did next, Goddamn, that's all I hope."

———

A guide of ours had a wife who appeared to be quite ill. Nobody seemed able to figure out just what the matter was, except she was exhausted all the time. He is reported to have said to her,

"By gar, I think there's somethin' in your blood that isn't there!"

———

A summer visitor walked into the local general store and asked the owner how business was.

He says, "Well, Monday I sold a case of sardines. Didn't do nuthin' Tuesday. Wednesday the fella brought back the case of sardines. So, I guess you could say Tuesday was my best day."

———

Guess it was the same fella who was asked if he had a certain article in stock.

"Nope."

"Why not?"

"Don't carry 'em any more—moved too fast."

When the foreman of the sardine factory in Yarmouth was asked how many men worked there, he sez, "'Bout half."

So much talk about town meetings these days, it reminds me of a long debate up-country about putting a new fence around the cemetery.

One of the older voters got up and said, "Don't make much sense to me. Nobody in there can get out, and nobody out wants to git in."

Some years back Ben Pritchard, driving his old pickup truck, went clean through a stoplight and smacked real hard, broadside, into a big Cadillac with New York plates. He really whaled it. The fellow from New York was some upset, got out, walked over to Ben, yelled and hollered, and gave him a real hard time.

When the New Yorker had finally blown off most of his steam, Ben said, "Now, young fella, there ain't no sense in you carryin' on like this. It ain't so bad!" He then opened the glove compartment, drew out a pint of whiskey he always kept there, and said, "Now, try a pull of this and calm down a bit." The fellow from New York took a long draw of the whiskey and handed it back to Ben, who promptly put the cork back in the pint and started to put it back in the glove compartment.

"Aren't you going to have some?" asked the New Yorker.

"Nope," sez Ben, "I'll wait till after the police come."

There was a Texan who drove into town one day, stopped to chat with a local farmer, and asked all kinds of questions about raising crops, watering, pest control, and so forth. Finally he asked how many acres were being worked. The farmer said, "Figger 'bout ten."

The fella from Texas said, "Well, on my farm, I start drivin' around it and don't get back to where I started for two hours."

The farmer said, "Yup, I had a truck like that once but got rid of it."

One day a fellow was drivin' a load of chickens to the processing plant. Every mile or so he'd stop the truck, get out, and belt the side of the truck with a baseball bat. A police cruiser finally stopped him. The trooper said, "I ain't stoppin' you to arrest you or nawthin', but I've been followin' you for fifteen minutes and I can't figure why every mile or so you stop and hit the side of your truck with the baseball bat."

"Well," the fellow said, "this here is a one-ton truck. I got three ton chicken aboard, so I got to keep two-thirds of 'em in the air all the time."

The tenth-grade teacher asked all in the class to write a poem, either original or one they'd heard. One young fellow wrote:

> As I was sitting in a shady nook
> Along beside a babbling brook,
> I saw a lovely little lass,
> Standing in water up to her knees.

The teacher said, "Johnny, that's fine, but it doesn't rhyme!"
"Well," sez Johnny, "we've had a mighty dry spring."

———

A friend of mine's sister once taught school in a real old one-room schoolhouse down east. One year, day after Labor Day, she was standing in the school yard to greet the new students. Up there in the potato country some of the kids didn't get around to school 'til maybe they were seven or eight years old. She spied one boy almost as tall as she was, put her arm around him, and said, "Well, I'll bet you know your ABC's."

He looked at her and said, "For Christ sake, I just got heah."

———

Seems Parson Jones came over from the rectory, washed up, and set down at the table for the evening meal. His good wife had spent most of the morning making a real fine stew of leftovers—some chunks of beef from Sunday's supper, some bits of chicken from Monday's dinner, and even the remains of a boiled ham. When the parson sat down he immediately dug in and started to eat. His amazed wife said, "Ain't you going to give the blessing?"

He said, "Already blessed it three times!"

———

Also heard that a while back the parson asked one of his parishioners if he'd "found Christ."

"Didn't know he was lost!"

———

To me a beautiful example of the State of Mainer's pride and independence is the following. My grandmother Sawyer was cooling doughnuts on the back stoop one summer at Little Chebeague. One of the young farm hands was passing by. Grandmother hollered, "Frank, want some doughnuts?"

"No thanks, ma'am, I git me vittles to home."

An outlander and his wife drivin' along stopped and asked an old-timer how to get to Millinocket.

He scratched his head and said, "Well, you turn 'round and go 'til you git to Ed Brown's silo. Take a left there and go 'bout five miles 'til you git to a red barn. Take a right there and go another three miles 'til you come to a cemetery. Take a left at the cemetery ... now, lemme see! Go straight there for—no! Gol darn it, you can't get there from here."

Another fellow in the middle of what appeared to be a small town asked the way to Dover-Foxcroft. The answer was, "Don't you move a Goddamned inch!"

Phil Doughty on Big Chebeague had a cow who was having her first calf. It was a powerful hot August day and his cow was bawlin' and carryin' on somethin' awful. Phil went out to help her and was sweatin' and workin' real hard pullin' on that calf's legs. Seems his son, age five or six, came runnin' out to the pasture and said, "Pop, want to ask you a question."

Phil said, "Go 'way, son, don't you see I'm busy as all get out helpin' this here cow?"

His son pestered Phil for some time, and finally Phil said, "All right, then, jest one question, and then git."

The boy said, "All I wanted to know is how fast was that calf runnin' when he hit that cow in the ass?"

"Think it's going to stop raining?"

"Always has."

While picking up his mail, a visitor from New Jersey said to the postmaster, "You sure got a lot of old folk up here. What's your mortality rate?"

"Just like it's always been ... one per person."

Some disappointed heirs of an eccentric old character were trying to break his will in a Maine court a few years back. The lawyer representing the heirs was trying hard to make a case that the testator had been incompetent.

"Did you ever hear this man talking to himself when he was alone?" he asked one of the testator's old cronies.

"Nope," said the old-timer, after giving the question a moment's thought. "Fact is, I was never with him when he was alone."

12

Oscar was driving his one-horse rig down Main Street when he spied Josh sitting in front of the village store whittling. Oscar drew up and said,
"How be ya?"
"Tolerable."
"How be your wife?"
"Betterin nawthin'!"

———

Another way this has been told:
Oscar says, "What's new?"
"Nawthin' much! Got a hoss for my wife."
"Damn good trade."

———

Arnie Belcher had told his hired hand, Ezekiel, to be at the Brownville Junction train station to meet him when he got back from ordering feed in Bangor. Zeke met him at the strike of four o'clock with the pickup and, without saying a word, sped them over Cedar Swamp Road on the way to the farm. With just two miles to go and not a word yet out of Zeke, Arnie decided something must be wrong.
"Anythin' atall happin while I was away?"
Zeke looked sheepishly to the floorboards and took fifteen whole seconds to answer.
"No, not much." he said quietly. "You did lose your mare."
"Lost my mare, did I?" said Arnie. "What from?"
"Burnt horseflesh," Zeke replied.
"Was the fire in my barn?"
"'Fraid so."
"What set the barn afire?"
"Sparks from the house."
"Godamighty, what set the house afire?"
"Folks say it was the drapes."
"For God's sake, what set the drapes ablaze?"
"Heard it was candles."
"Where in Sam Hill was the candles?"
"On the casket."

13

"WHOSE CASKET?"

"Your Aunt Flossie's."

"Jesus, how did Flossie die?"

"Shock, I s'pose."

"What in God's name shocked her to death?"

"I s'pose it was when your wife ran off with the postmasteh."

"You feeling better?"

"Betterin what?"

"You got a criminal lawyer over your way?"

"We think so, but we haven't been able to prove nawthin' on him yet."

"Heard your wife just had a baby."

"Yup."

"'Twas it a boy or a girl?"

"We weren't sure for awhile, but it turned out to be a boy."

"Nice looking baby, is it?"

"Fred, I'll tell ya, if you gave me a stick of white pine and a sharp knife, I could have whittled you a better lookin' baby."

The constable lost so much money in the stock market, he decided to end it all. He drove into town and bought a bottle of carbolic acid, a can of gasoline, a length of strong rope, and a big hoss pistol. He threw one end of the rope over the branch of the tree that hangs out over the river and tied the other end of the rope around his neck. Then he swallowed the carbolic acid, doused himself with gasoline, and lit it. He kicked off the bank and swung out over the river, puttin' that big hoss pistol to his head. He fired and missed and severed the rope instead. He plunged into the water, which doused the flames. He then swallowed so much

14

water that he coughed up all the carbolic acid. "And, you know, if he hadn't been such a darned good swimmer, he woulda drowned."

———

"How far is it to Kennebunkport?"
"'Bout 26,000 miles, the way you're going."

———

One of the most suspicionin' folks in all Maine was a fellow named Noah who lived near Sabbathday Pond. One day his uncle up and died and left him $127.73. Noah never set much store in banks, but there was no place else to cash the check. The teller fellow counted out 127 dollars, bill by bill, and 73 cents, coin by coin, and then Noah did the same, lookin' suspicious-like.
"What's the matter?" asked the teller, "It's right, ain't it?"
"Yup," muttered Noah, "but just barely."

———

"You know the story about the two old ladies from Meddy-bemps?"

"No, not lest you can remember their names."

———

One old gal, attending the interment of old Ned Pickett at a burial ground quite a fur piece from town, said to another old lady, "How old be you now?"

"Nigh on to eighty-eight," she said.

The first old lady replied, "I'm pushing eighty-seven myself. Hardly pays us to walk back to town!"

———

An old gent in a cracker-barrel store walked over to a neighbor he had hardly spoken a word to in years and said, "What did you give your hoss when she had the glonders?"

"Kerosene," he replied.

Meeting again the following week, they resumed the conversation. "What did you tell me you gave your hoss when she had the glonders?"

Again, "Kerosene" was the answer.

"Well, I did that and my horse DIED."

"So'd mine."

———

A young lad down Greenville way who was just starting out fox trapping went to the best known trapper in Piscataquis County and offered him $25 for his secret to success. After the sap began to flow and the season was over, the old trapper went up to the lad one day in the post office and said,

"How'd you make out trappin' this wintah?"

"Not good a bit," the lad replied. "Caught nary a one."

"Did you use the secret I give ya?"

"Nope," said the boy, "I found me a better way."

———

A young farmhand was bailing down Cedar Swamp Road in his pickup truck one afternoon headin' for Norridgewalk, when Fred Fowler's Guernsey cow sauntered across the road. He belted her right smart in the stern, sending her sprawling into a ditch. The cow, only shaken up a mite, wriggled her way back to her feet. The lad, heaving a sigh, wandered nearby where Mr. Fowler was working his vegetable patch.

"She looks okay to me," said the boy nervously. "I don't think I done her any harm."

Whereupon Fred replied, "Sonny, if you think you done her any good, I'd be glad to pay ya for it!"

A spell later, another of Fred's cows was less fortunate. Fred was obliged, for the first time in his life, to fill out an insurance form. Under the item "Disposition of Carcass" he wrote, "Kind and gentle."

Emily Wiggins was sittin' with her sister, Bessie, in the family pew at the Mere Point Methodist Church one Sunday morning when the preacher said, "We've got to 'radicate all sin." She whispered, "Amen." When he said, "We've got to 'liminate all tabaccer," she said, "Amen, amen!" When he said, "We're gonna 'radicate all liquor," she said, "Now, Bessie, he's meddlin'."

Now there aren't but a couple of Democrats in the whole State of Maine. One year, Floss Pennel walked into the town clerk's office in South Paris and said,

"Want to change my registration from Republican to Democrat."

"Land's sake, Floss, you can't do a thing like that. Why the Pennels have been Republican for generations."

"I know it," said Floss. "But I aim to change anyway."

"Why in Sam Hill would you ever do a thing like that?"

"Well," replied Floss, "I'm pushin' ninety and I figger I haven't got too long to go, but when I do go, I'd rather it be one of them than one of us."

Homer Drinkwater and Al Trefethen were tearing out a real old chimney in Al's house. They had to get a pile of those chimney bricks off the attic floor and down cellar.

"You know, Al," said Homer, "those old bricks are worth a powerful lot of money. So load 'em into the barrel easy-like, and get a rope around that barrel. Now run it through the pulley on the rafters above you, and pass it down to me in the cellar. Now you ease that barrel to the edge of the attic floor, and I'll haul on the rope from this end."

Well, when Al swung the barrel off the attic floor into the air, it apparently weighed more than Homer, 'cause it headed down, and he headed up. The barrel met him halfway and took a good deal of him with it. When he refused to let go, he jammed his fingers in the pulley and bounced his head off the rafter. When the barrel hit the cellar floor, the bricks came out of the bottom of it, and then he must of weighed more'n the barrel 'cause it headed up, and he headed down.

When he met the barrel halfway again, what it didn't do to him in the first place, it did in the second. Homer landed so hard on the cellar floor that he let go of the rope, and the barrel came down and hit him on the head. When he came to, he was inside the barrel settin' on top of a pile of broken bricks.

"Al," said Homer, "that should be a lesson to the both of us. Seems to me, when you try to hold onto somethin' of value these days, through all the ups and downs, chances are betterin fifty-fifty you're gonna wind up in a barrel."

———

Two Frenchmen, while logging up by the border, took a day off to go bear hunting. After almost a full day without seeing even a track, one turned to the other and said,

"Where de bar?"

"I tink he hiboornating."

"How he do that?"

"He jess crawl in a deep hole and stay there all winter."

"What he do in thar?"

"He jess sit and lick his paw."

"I bet his paw like that."

———

18

Another Frenchman was planking his boat while another watched him. The fellow doing the planking would pick up a nail, look at it, and then drive it home. Then he'd look at another one and throw it over his shoulder. Seems as if every fifth or sixth nail he'd throw over his shoulder. Finally, the fellow watching said,

"Why you throw them over your shoulder?"

"Point on the wrong end."

"By gar, I tink you crazy. You could use them on the other side."

———

One day, up Farmington way, old Josh Drummond got real worried about his old buddy, Amos. Of late, Amos looked some peaked and didn't seem as pert as usual.

Josh persuaded Amos to go with him to see Old Doc Johnson. The Doc looked him over real good, said there wa'nt much matter with him. Give him a few pills and asked him to leave ten dollars on the side table on the way out.

When they got out on the front stoop, old Amos fell face down dead as a haddock. Josh went back in and told Doc what happened. Doc thought a minute and then said:

"Well, I'll be danged! Tell you what, though, on your way out would you mind turning him around so he'll look like he was comin' in?"

Up in St. Raymond in the Province, a resident was real upset with a neighbor's boy who continually ran through his yard on the way to school.

One day the owner fetched ahold of him and said, "Next time you run through my yard, you go 'round."

The widow Abbey Skolfield went out one cold winter day for her regular constitutional. While walking around Craig's Pond, she spied a young boy floundering around in a hole in the ice.

She walked out on the ice, stretched a birch sapling to the hole, and pulled him out. The boy was so cold and exhausted, he couldn't walk. Being a large, strong gal, she threw him over her shoulder and carried him over a mile back to his house. Entering the house, she laid the boy down on the couch and said to the boy's mother,

"Found him nigh unto drowning in the pond."

"Thank ye, Abbey, where's his mittens?"

A pickup truck was down to its axles in mud. A fellow said to the owner,

"Looks like she be mired real good."

"She ain't 'til I try to pull her out."

The editor of the Portland *Press Herald* sent a reporter up to Jonesport to interview a spinster who was reported to be the oldest inhabitant of Washington County. In endeavoring to find out to what the gal attributed her longevity, the reporter asked,

"Do you smoke?"

"Used to."

"Drink?"

"Been known to."

"Exercise?"

"Mostly walking to the zoo."

"Diet?"

"Always et what I war amind to."

"Sick much?"

"Nope."

"In your ninety-eight years, haven't you ever been bedridden?"

"No," she said with her eyes gleaming, "but I had it once in a dory."

My good friend Bob Johnson was driving back from the Bridgton County Fair with his boy. At about North Windham he came to a fork in the road. Each road had a sign to Portland. Spying a young fellow trudging along, Bob drew up alongside of him, rolled down the window and hollered, "Make any difference which road I take to Portland?"

Without glancing up the boy said, "Not to me it don't."

"Why you look so glum, John?"

"Shot my dog."

"Was he mad?"

"Well, he warn't too damn pleased."

A couple of lobster fishermen were discussing the various merits of a Maine-built hull versus a Novi Hull as one of them was needing a new boat.

One said to the other who felt the price of a Novi boat was far less, "Hell no, Captain, you don't want one of them Novi Boats. They is built of hackmatack by beavers with dull teeth. Only thing that keeps 'em together is termites holdin' hands."

Up in Kennebunk my Bowdoin classmate Hartley Lord heard that Milt Webber was in jail up in Eliot for murder. He went over to the harbor to find out what had happened. Found a friend of Milt's and said, "Hear Milt's in the slammer in Eliot. What in hell happened?"

"Well," says the fella, "Milt come home last night late. Goes upstairs and found a fella in bed with his wife. Shot 'em both dead. But," he says, "could of been worse."

"How could it of been worse? Two people dead and Milt probably on his way to be."

"Well, if it'd been last night, coulda' been me."

21

On the top step of the country store sat an old gaffer with a very large police dog stretched out at his feet. A fella starting up the steps paused and inquired, "Your dog bite?"

"Nope," came the reply.

The fella started up, and the dog growled and went for him. With no damage done, the fella said, "Thought you allowed that your dog don't bite!"

"He don't," came the reply, "but that ain't my dog."

Some years ago, I was walking down the main street in Bethel. It was a glorious January-thaw day with a foot of slush on the sidewalk.

I said to a fellow coming toward me, "Kind of rough going underfoot, but sure is great overhead."

He sez, "Yup, but I ain't going that way."

He who laughs, lasts.

GLOSSARY

The Glossary contains not only terms used in the text but also some whaling terms, and others, that have interested me over the years.

To bail To move fast; to "bail along." To take water out of a boat; to "bail the dory."

Bitter end There is never a rope on a sailing craft, always a line. The end of a line that did not have a loop spliced into it was called the "bitter end."

Bone in her teeth Vessel at good speed, throwing white bow wake (wave). Really pushing water!

The cat Whip, often with metal ends, used to lash and punish a seaman. A "cat o' nine tails" was nine leather thongs. Many seamen died by the "cat."

Chumslick An oily slick made by cutting up, or even grinding up, fish bait and tossing it off the stern while the boat is anchored. Wind and tide will drift the pieces of fish and oil far astern. The large game fish will follow the slick right up to the boat and hopefully be hooked on the lines floated off the stern. The practice is called chumming.

Davy Jones's locker Floor of the ocean. Buried in "Davy Jones's locker."

Dory A double-ended skiff, tender, or small rowboat, lapstraked, or planked with the lower side of each plank overlapping the next. The "Banks dory" was used on the Grand Banks with two men hand lining for codfish. As many as twenty Banks dories, usually eighteen feet long, were used from off the "mother schooner." The "Swampscott dory" was somewhat shorter and had finer lines than the Banks dory from Maine and Nova Scotia.

Down east The prevailing wind along the New England coast is from the southwest. It blows in a northeast direction. Therefore, sailing vessels sailed downwind from Boston to Portland, or "down east." Returning, one had to beat, or tack, upwind all the way. It was therefore "up" to Boston. Inland and away from the shore in Maine, it is different. If, say, you lived in South Paris, it would be going "down" to Portland and "up" to Bangor; sideways it is "to" Camden and "to" Fryeburg; close by you would go "over" to Harrison.

Famine Farming.

To fetch To get or get to. "Fetch" a pail of water. "Fetch" port.

Finest kind The best, great! How's the weather? the new pump? fishing? the new baby? Anything that was real good was "finest kind."

Gallied Without muffled oars and quiet, whales would frighten easily and go off in all directions or "sound" (dive deep); that is, they would be "gallied."

Gam To talk, exchange news, or just chat. When two whaling vessels would meet far out to sea (maybe one returning to New Bedford or another home port after a four-year cruise, and the other on the way to the whaling grounds), they would come alongside each other, mix crews, exchange letters and news, maybe have some grog, and, in short, have a "gam."

Game Sore or crippled. "Game" leg.

Glass Barometer. The "glass" is low or falling. Bad weather!

Grog 1/3 rum, 2/3 water.

Hand Seaman. All "hands" on deck.

Head Toilet on modern boats. The whalers had no toilets. A plank hung from davits over the water on the leeward side served the purpose.

Heft The weight or sometimes truth. What's the "heft" of that?

Hogshead Large barrel containing seventeen bushels of flour, biscuits (hardtack), salt pork, and so forth.

Honey barrel On whaling vessels a large barrel was always lashed to the foot of the foremast. All members of the crew would urinate in the barrel. After "cutting in" and "trying out" a whale by boiling the blubber, all hands were covered with oil, and rigging, decks, and clothing were covered with soot and oil; all were washed in the contents of the "honey barrel." The tanic acid did the job. The clothes were then dragged overboard, and in a day all was "shipshape and Bristol fashion"—everything clean again. (Honey Fitz was not called Honey because of his sweetness but because as a youth he drove a garbage wagon that smelled and dripped pretty rotten stuff.)

24

Honk To move fast. "Honk it to her."

To horse To pull hard. A fish well hooked can be "horsed in."

In the doldrums Becalmed. No wind. One of the worst places for the doldrums was Sargasso Sea, halfway from the Azores to South America on the equator. Vessels were without any breeze for weeks, even months. If a man is "in the doldrums," he is "pretty low."

To iron To sink a harpoon into whale, swordfish, or tuna.

Keelhaul Severe (and many times fatal) punishment for a seaman. Tied by two lines—one on hands, one on feet—and pulled the length of a vessel under the keel. Usually ripped apart by barnacles.

The Old Man The skipper or captain, whether twenty or sixty years old.

Outlander A down-east expression for "city folk" or "out-of-staters."

Painter Line at the bow of a dory, skiff, or whaleboat for towing or tying up at a pier or dock.

Peaked Pronounced PEA-kid. To look worn out, tired. A fellow looked "a mite peaked."

Pod School of whales, tuna, bluefish—any concentration of fish.

Rimwracked When dragging for fish, if the net got caught on a ledge or an old wreck and got all torn up, the crew would say they had been "rimwracked." A fellow who looked or felt all beat up was "rimwracked."

Scaling up The fog is lifting, or "scaling up."

Scuttlebutt Water was scarce. A large barrel of water, the "scuttlebutt," was kept at the foot of the mainmast. Tin cups hung on nails around the mast. Here the crew—some from fore, some from aft—would meet and exchange gossip, rumors, news, and so forth; hence, what's the "scuttlebutt"?

Son of a gun In the early 1800's when the British Navy was noted for its brutality to seamen, it was necessary to shanghai (kidnap) boys and men from the farms to obtain a crew. After a three- or four-year cruise, when the vessel returned to port, the crew was not allowed ashore for fear of desertion. Hence, while the vessel was being fitted out and reprovisioned for a new voyage, women would be brought aboard, grog served, and a party held, always on the gun deck. Many a child was conceived under a gun; hence the term "son of a gun."

Sperm whale The only whale with teeth, and then only on the lower jaw.

To splice the main brace To have a ration of rum or grog.

Stove in Vessel rammed. Hole in hull. A hurt man can be "all stove in."

Thirteen Most early colonial New England homes had rooms 13' x 13' from corner post to corner post. Thirteen was considered lucky. There were thirteen original states. The national emblem, the eagle, has thirteen olive branches in its right claw, thirteen arrows in its left claw, and thirteen feathers in its tail. The British started the rumor that thirteen was unlucky.

Waif Tall marker, a flag on a pole attached to a line to a swordfish, or stuck in a drifting whale. A youngster called a waif is drifting through life.

Warp Bring a vessel alongside a dock or pier. A "light line." To "warp alongside."

To whale To hit hard.

Zoo Outhouse or privy.